A Truly Unexpected Life Story

Published by
HenschelHAUS Publishing, Inc.
Milwaukee, Wisconsin
www.henschelHAUSbooks.com

ISBN: 97989912791-8-5
LCCN: 2024950187
E-book and audio book also available.

Cover photos (courtesy of the author):

- Patch for one of 15 communication satellites that Ford Aerospace built in the 1970s and '80s. Intelsat was a conglomeration of 103 nations, all of whom had access to the technology.

- Photo of the author working on one of the early IntelSat V series satellites.

- The author, with his younger brother Terry, climbed and descended the back side of Half Dome, Yosemite National Park, CA, in record time.

Printed in the United States of America

I dedicate this book to my wife, Marie.

For 52 years, she's stuck with me in good times and hard times. More than once over the years, I've preached that God sees us the way we REALY are, deep inside, and He loves us still.

Marie has seen me and knows me like nobody else knows me ... and she loves me still.
In my valleys of depression, and on mountaintop experiences, her love has been a rock for me.
It has never wavered, never faltered.
She is God's incredible gift to a man who truly doesn't deserve her.

A TRULY UNEXPECTED LIFE STORY

I graduated in the 1970 class of Milwaukee Hamilton high school with a mind-boggling 1.9 grade point average. This placed me squarely in the middle of the bottom quarter of the class of 975 students. Not much to write home about.

If the story had ended there, it would have been a sad story indeed. But my story becomes something of a wonder to me and a great surprise to many.

Within ten years of high school graduation, I was placed in a position as test conductor in charge of lunch operations at Cape Canaveral Florida for Ford Aerospace located in Palo Alto California. We built what were at the time the largest communication satellites in space. I went to work there to pay off some college debt. I began as a low-level technician. I enjoyed the work, I worked hard, listened to what I was told to do, and moved up the corporate ladder fairly quickly.

When I traveled from our home in Sunnyvale, California to the San Francisco Airport I was driven by a chauffeur in a limousine each time I traveled. People on the freeway would strain to see who was sitting in the back of the limo. (Maybe a movie star?) The windows were tinted dark and they couldn't see in. I felt myself wanting to roll down the window, wave and say, "It's just me...I'm nobody."

I had a beautiful three-bedroom condo right on Cocoa Beach. It was hard work with long hours but it was a fairly glamorous lifestyle. Young sailors would snap to attention to open the door to the highbay area where we did final testing. I was 28 years old with a degree in theology working with some of the most brilliant aerospace minds on the planet. How strange I thought that before they could approach the spacecraft they had to get the nod from the 28-year-old cop's son from Milwaukee.

In my life, I have been blessed with a number of things I could never have anticipated. In this book, I will share with you some of the amazing things I had the honor of being part of, including leading a group of ten therapists, chaplains, and pastors to do crisis counseling and debriefings with police officers in New Orleans after Hurricane Katrina.

I will share with you some of the things we saw and heard there that were never broadcast on national news. I hope this book will keep you entertained. I hope you'll be encouraged, strengthened, challenged. I trust it will bring you a good belly laugh from time to time. The stories I tell will be short, true, and I hope they help make your day. Most of them I wrote to family and friends on Facebook to encourage and help them.

Welcome to *A Truly Unexpected Life Story*.

WE CHANGED A NATION

For years, the nation of India suffered at the hands of mighty tropical cyclones (hurricanes) that devastated its coasts. Countless lives were lost because there was simply no way to warn the people of impending deadly storms.

Insat 1 changed that.

Ford Aerospace in Palo Alto, California built a series of three satellites that helped the people of India forecast impending landfalls, many days in advance. I had the honor of working as test conductor on all three of the series. With the capacity to not only detect their weather, Insat also transmitted two TV stations and ten thousand phone lines. Thousands of towns and villages were now able to receive live satellite classroom education where there had been none across much of the country. It literally changed the history of education in India.

Being part of that whole process is one of the highlights of my time at Ford Aerospace. We truly helped change a nation.

LIKE ONE OF MY KIDS

I had the great joy of watching all three of our children come into the world by Caesarean section. The smallest was our third, Benjamin, who came in at 9 pounds 2 ounces. Ryan and Julie were 9 pounds 7 and 9 pounds 5, respectively. It was such a powerful time watching each of them breathe their first breath. It's something you just never forget.

I experienced something that comes in a close second, though. Near the end of 1984, while we lived in Oconto, Wisconsin, I watched as the first night-launched Space Shuttle blasted off from Cape Canaveral. It was STS 8, the eighth in line of the shuttle launches. It was just after midnight in Wisconsin as I watched national TV show the cargo bay doors open ever so slowly. My heart was beating in my throat as I watched the long delivery arm lift Inset 1B slowly from the cargo area, some 200 miles above Earth.

This was a very complicated payload. I had worked countless hours as a test conductor during the assembly of all three of the Insat series. It carried capacity for 10,000 phone lines, two TV stations, and the first of its kind with a very accurate weather camera on board. It was called a Very High-Resolution Reflectometer (VHRR) and helped predict deadly impending weather days in advance of landfall. Its own 100-pound rocket thruster blasted it out to geo-stationary (geosynchronous) orbit 22,300 miles above the equator. This was truly one of the highlights of my entire life and I count it a huge honor to have been a part of it. It was one of my kids!

THE LOVE OF A FATHER

I stood on the other side of the glass, looking at the face of our first-born, Ryan David Carlson. I knew tears of joy were streaming down my face as my emotions overflowed. He was a miracle. My wife, Marie, and I had been married for more than eight years and were not sure we could even have children. Now, as I stared at Ryan's face, I heard God's voice. It was not audible, but it was deep and profound and went right to my heart. "Now you're beginning to feel how much I really love you." That was 25 years ago, but the impact of His words has never left me.

Over the next three years, with rare exception, when I was not at work, Ryan was my shadow. We went to ball games together, to the park, played in the yard. We truly adored each other. Then, just before his third birthday, tragedy struck. I received the message in my office at Ford Aerospace in Palo Alto, CA. Marie had been involved in an accident. I called the hospital and found out Marie, and Julie, our one-year-old, were both fine. But Ryan was in very critical condition. The impact of the head-on collision caused his head to snap forward, severing his brain stem. The prognosis was very grim. The EEG showed minimal brain activity. If he lived, it would be with machines attached. He would be paralyzed and unable to function on his own. Three days later, God took him home and spared us the decision of whether to keep him alive with machines.

All of my study and seminary training could not prepare us for this. We needed someone much greater than ourselves to see us through this awful trauma. God held us powerfully, tenderly, and closely. Without His supernatural presence, we would not have made it.

God spoke many things to us in those days—sometimes through family or friends; sometimes directly to our hearts.

About two weeks after Ryan died, I was crying out to God alone one afternoon. He reminded me of what He'd spoken to me three years earlier, the day Ryan was born. I remembered those words: "Now you're beginning to feel how much I love you." But now Ryan was gone. No one could possibly understand this grief. That's when God spoke again: "Now you're truly beginning to understand how much I love you."

I knew immediately what God meant. He did understand my grief. He did understand our loss. He watched as His Son died. That was a true reflection of His incredible love. The impact of His word has remained a part of me to this day. Who can truly understand the love of a father, the Father, who willingly gave his Son. What else could He possibly do to demonstrate His love for mankind? "For God so loved the world that He gave His only begotten son..."

I believe I never understood grief until that time. After that time, I never viewed grief in the same way. I believe Marie and I went to the very depths of grief. I cannot describe it adequately. Neither can I adequately describe the breadth and depth of God's love and presence, particularly in our valley experience.

God's word was a constant source of strength and help in those difficult days. Verses like Heb. 13:5, "For He Himself has said, 'I will never leave you or forsake you'" took on a new and personal meaning for us. "Lo, I am with you always, even to the end of the earth: (Mt. 28:20) was a verse that reached out to us like a life-saving ring to person overboard in rough seas. For us, we were truly at the end of the earth. He was there. Ryan's death was not the only tragedy we faced at that time. Marie's dad had passed away before Ryan died. A few months after Ryan's death, Marie miscarried.

During this time, our intimacy with God deepened. Our reliance on Him deepened. Our appreciation of His sacrifice deepened. I believe our love for people deepened. I know our sense of empathy with those in grief deepened considerably.

As I minister, I believe I understand what it means to be a wounded healer. We have been deeply wounded, but by God's grace, we've been able to touch many lives out of our pain. We found God's grace and presence even in the darkest times, and we've been able to share that personal experience in many ways over the years.

(Article published in the *Pentacostal Evangel*)
Woodland Worship Center, Oneida, WI

Ryan David Carlson

DEATHLY EMBARRASSED

Pretty smart?? More like pretty embarrassed. I never received higher than a B in Spanish in all the eight years I studied it from fifth grade through twelfth in the Milwaukee public school system. However, I became fluent in Spanish. I then learned to speak fairly fluent Portuguese at the cheese factory I worked at in Los Banos, California. Several of the men working there were from Mexico and Portugal and so some days, I spoke predominantly Spanish and Portuguese.

In college, I studied both Greek and Hebrew. Because Greek is one of the romantic languages, I learned it fairly readily. Hebrew is much different and was more difficult to grasp. When I took notes during class, my notes were written in English, Spanish, or Greek, depending on which word was shortest in that language.

I'm really not trying to sound terribly impressive. My capacity to learn languages was borne out of some terribly painful and embarrassing years in my life. As a kid, my parents had me attend speech therapy for years because I had what I thought was a very terrible speech impediment. I said words with the letter "S"out of the far-right side of my mouth. I went to a speech therapist once a week for years. When I'd get up from my desk to head down the hall to the therapist's office, one wise guy in the class would always loudly ask, "Hey, Carlson, where you going?"

I was terribly embarrassed to speak in public....ever. I got into the habit of forming sentences with words that did not contain the letter S. My brain was constantly going 100 miles an hour thinking about words just out of self-preservation. I focused on words to avoid being laughed and snickered at.

I was 12 and playing baseball with some buddies on a hot August afternoon. Playing center field, I started saying S's out of the center of my mouth rather than the right side. The speech therapist had tried to get me to do this for years. I just kept repeating the letter S over and over again. Thank God, I continued to say the letter S correctly.

My habit of thinking about words thankfully went from painful to productive. Languages became an easy thing for me to grasp. I have conducted many weddings in Spanish and English. Twice, I was hired to travel all the way to Chicago to perform weddings in both Spanish and English because they couldn't find anybody closer to do them. Romans 8:28 truly tells my story. "And we know that all things work together for good to them that love Him."

What was terribly painful, what was embarrassing, what was very, very difficult, turned into something positive and productive that has helped me throughout the rest of my life.

THE MOUSE THAT ROARED

He screamed bloody murder. It was my younger brother Terry—and older brother David and I were terrified something awful had happened to him.

The story: The three Carlson brothers were playing golf at the Whitnall Park golf course on Milwaukee's southwest side. David and I were then and always will be duffers. A "duffer"is a really untalented golfer in golf-speak. A 200-yard drive was a dream for us.

Terry, on the other hand, was an awesome golfer, just as he was in all sports. He regularly smashed the ball 300 yards plus down the fairway. This day was no different. David and I struggled to play bogey or double bogey golf. Terry was smashing it farther than our eyes could follow.

On this particular hole, David and I had hit the ball three times to get as far as Terry's first drive. We had managed to stay on the fairway at least. Terry had hooked his 300-yard monster drive into the deep grass on the left side of the fairway (called "the rough"). David and I were analyzing where our next pathetic hits would be when we heard the blood-curdling scream.

Terry was in complete panic mode and I suspect people heard his screams two miles away back at the clubhouse. We ran to his side. He was absolutely mortified. Something had crawled under the cuff of his blue jeans and was crawling all the way up his leg. Terry was smashing his leg to assassinate whatever the monster was. He dropped his jeans all the way to the ground and stood there in the middle of the fairway in his Fruit of the Looms.

David and I were absolutely frantic for our little brother. Then we saw it. From the bottom of his pants cuff fell a tiny 5- or 6-ounce brown field mouse. It was terrified at the attempted assassination of his little field mouse life. It fled, not running forward. It kind of half-hopped sideways back into the tall grass to tell his mommy about his horrible ordeal.

It took us several seconds to grasp what had taken place. That little mouse had run all the way up Terry's leg with those sharp little mouse claws. Then the utter hilarity hit David and me. Honestly, we laughed so hard we couldn't breathe. We fell on the ground holding our stomachs in loud, uproarious laughter. Terry was still trying to grasp the attempt on his life. We tried to finish our golf game but the image of that tiny mouse kept us in hysterics the remainder of the afternoon.

Funny how insignificant things can play on our fears, don't you think?

SERMON WITH NO WORDS

True story.

It was an upper middle-class church where most of the men wore ties and most of the women wore dresses and authentic jewelry, pearls, diamond bracelets, and so on. The church was full as usual on Sunday morning. They had already sung the hymns and the pastor was about to begin his sermon.

Then it happened.

From the back of the sanctuary, a man started to walk down the center aisle, looking for a seat. Nobody moved over to make room for him. Further and further toward the front of the church he slowly walked. Still, nobody moved. They just did not want him sitting next to them. After all, he had long hair flowing half way down his back. Even worse, his clothes were dirty and full of holes. He looked as though he hadn't had a shower in some time. He walked all the way up the center aisle because he couldn't find a seat anywhere.

Finally, with every eye looking at him, he just sat down on the floor, right next to the front pew. People gasped. *How awful*, many thought. What was this dirty hippie doing in their church!!??

The drama continued. From the back of the sanctuary walked the head usher. He'd held that position for many years. What would he do with the dirty hippie? Because of his age, he couldn't walk fast. He was always dressed in a sharp suit. A very dapper gentleman.

Then, the head usher did the unthinkable. He walked up to the young man and sat down right next to him on the floor. That's where he remained for the rest of the service.

After the service, one man was heard to say, "I may not remember the sermon the pastor preached...but I'll never forget the sermon that old head usher preached this morning."

ONCE IN A LIFETIME

Once in a lifetime? I was driving back to Green Bay from our cabin just outside Lake Tomahawk, WI. I had turned left onto Hwy. 47 on the edge of town, then a right turn onto Co. D, just a quarter mile from town. It was a bright, clear morning when I saw a beautiful, dark-furred deer just 200 or so yards ahead of me, walking slowly from my right to left across the road.

After driving in Wisconsin for many years, I still love seeing deer in the wild. I couldn't tell if it was a doe or buck from that distance. I had pulled about 150 yards away now. I was trying to see if it had antlers. I was so focused on his head that I pretty much ignored his tail. Then I looked closer.

It had a really long tail for a deer. I heard myself say out loud, "That's no deer—that's a stinkin' mountain lion!!"

Now I was just 30 or 40 yards from him. He turned and looked me squarely in the eyes, still walking at a very slow pace. I had goose pimples on goose pimples. It was like he was saying, "What, you've never seen a mountain lion before!??"

It was an encounter between just me and that beautiful cat. It was an awesome day for me.

CLIMBING A LEGEND

The campsites were full at Yosemite's Valley camp areas. That meant Marie, my younger brother Terry, and I had to spend one night camped in one of the higher elevation campsites, then head down to the valley to wait for a campsite to become available. Our plan was to set up a campsite early, then younger brother and I would walk the 10- to 12-hour hike up the back side of the famous 5,000-foot granite mountain, Half Dome.

Seen in movies, photos, artwork, and on sporting apparel around the world, Half Dome is one of the most recognizable sites on the planet. Our plan had to be modified because we had to wait until about 10 a.m. for a campsite. We finally began the 16-mile round-trip trek up a steep trail that took us some 5,000 feet up from Yosemite Valley.

Park rangers told us to plan for at least 10 to 12 hours each way. To say we were unprepared would be an understatement. People had told us that we'd have access to water on virtually the entire hike thanks to the Merced River, which runs next to the trail. What they didn't tell us was that the trail separated from the river about two-thirds of the way up. All we took along for water was a 16-oz. Tupperware cup with a lid. How dumb was that, you ask!!! Pretty dumb!!

The temperature at valley level was 100°F that day, with no breeze. Because of our very late start, we determined we'd have to make the climb in well under 10 to 12 hours. We were both in excellent shape back then. I ran six miles/day and Terry had played quarterback at U.W. La Crosse. I read later that hiking Half Dome was the equivalent of walking up 473 flights of stairs. We made it up the 11-hour climb in 4 1/2 hours.

The last 800 feet are almost vertical. There are metal pipes sticking out of the rock with cables at the ends so climbers can pull themselves upward. When we got to the top, we both collapsed. Our water was long gone. Terry's lips and mouth were snow white, like you'd see in a movie. It was probably one of the most dangerous predicaments I've ever been in.

Nine or ten climbers were at the top with us. Two of them offered us some weed. We declined but asked if they had any extra water. "Sorry, no."

In time, we walked over to the north face, sat and dangled our feet over the face looking down some 5,000 feet at the valley floor below. It was a once-in-a-lifetime moment.

After we spent several minutes drinking in the incredible view, we began walking around the top of the dome. What happened next, we both knew was a miracle. Sitting alone was a one-gallon plastic milk jug, half filled with liquid. Terry put a drop on his arm to taste. "Yuck, it's salt water!!"

It took a few moments for us to determine it wasn't salt water, but rather fresh water with salt from his arm. We shared the contents, which were the same 100°F as the air. It still tasted incredible!! It was enough to get us back down the trail to fresh water.

Daylight was slipping away quickly and we didn't want to be on the trail after dark for several practical reasons, including some with really big teeth. We ran the entire eight miles back to camp in exactly 2 1/2 hours. We tore the shreds out of our legs, leaving it impossible to walk for three days. Marie was not a happy camper. But we had climbed Half Dome and it was worth every step!

HE JUST SAID NO

"No, you're not going!"

I was 17, had my own Triumph motorcycle, thought I was tough as nails, and wanted to go to a weekend rock concert 60 miles north of Milwaukee. When I told my dad about my plans, his answer was as blunt as it was final. "You're not going to that concert...that's the end of it."I was frustrated, disappointed, confused, and not a little ticked off.

"Why not?"I reasoned with myself. "I'm almost out of high-school. I'm not going to do anything too stupid or reckless. Probably have a few beers."(At 17, I passed for 21 and never got carded) It just didn't make sense but I knew way better than to tangle with my tough, police sergeant dad. His word really was the final word!

Skip ahead two weeks. It was on the local news. Two fierce motorcycle gangs both showed up at the weekend concert. My ears perked up when the news anchor mentioned the concert by name. Then I got the chills. There had been violent war between the two gangs, right there where I was determined to go but couldn't. Not only were there knives, clubs, brass knuckles and so on, but a horrible gunfight broke out and terrified the concert goers. A bunch of people, including innocent bystanders, were shot—some criticality, some fatally.

My dad simply knew something I didn't. I hated the answer: NO. Dear friends, if there's one thing I know about our Heavenly Father, it's that sometimes He just says NO. We're determined to do something or go somewhere, even if we feel strongly about it. But He knows the future as well as the past. Have you matured enough in your Christian walk to say: "OK God. I don't really understand why you gave me this answer. But I'm confident in your wisdom and love for me. And I'm OK with this, God.

KATRINA'S UNTOLD STORIES

It was one of the worst natural disasters to ever hit America. It continued to build in intensity and ferocity in the Caribbean for several days before hitting landfall on August 29th, 2005. She was an all-consuming, ferocious monster, bent on destroying everything in her path. She was horribly effective.

National news coverage allowed us to be there without being there. We watched thousands fleeing their homes. Some victims lost much; many lost everything. In the days that followed we watched as people shared the heartache and misery resulting from Katrina's wrath.

A number of the members of my family were police officers and so I had particular interest as I listened to police officers being interviewed. For a time, I served as chaplain for the Brown County Sheriff's Department here in Green Bay. I have a special personal interest in police officers and the work they do.

"Does nobody else see that these guys are not doing okay?" I asked myself as I listened to police interviews. I remember praying, "God, somebody needs to help these guys!" I prayed that more than once. It was several days after Katrina that I felt a silent tap on my shoulder. I felt God was speaking very clearly to me when He said, "You go, and I'll be with you each step of the way."

I began the process of hand-picking nine highly qualified people, therapists, police and hospital chaplains, pastors—people I knew would be able to stand strong to be a great help to the officers in New Orleans. A friend of mine's sister was engaged to one of the leaders of Franklin Graham's disaster response team

Samaritan's Purse. She was instrumental in facilitating the door being opened for us.

We raised the money to head south and spent 11 days walking, talking, and listening. When we got there, the people from Samaritan's Purse took us aside and told us that we ten from Wisconsin were the first they were allowing in to work with the police officers in New Orleans. I understood exactly what they were saying. "This is huge. Don't blow it!!"

We broke into pairs, each pair working with one of the five precincts that weren't flooded out. My partner Pastor Randy Mantik and I covered the 8th precinct, which is the station that covers the French Quarter. We went to roll call each day at 5 PM, then walked the half block to Bourbon Street, where we listened as police unloaded some of the terrible burdens they were carrying. In this book, I share some of the stories we heard first-hand during those 11 days in Louisiana. Some stories I cannot share to this day.

On the trip home, we stopped for dinner and I asked those who were with me, "Does anybody feel that you might have been part of saving lives there?"To a person, they agreed that their time pouring into those brave officers probably saved a number of them from dangerous decisions, including suicide. That was sadly the way a number of them escaped the trauma that followed Katrina. It was one of the best eleven-day investments I've made in my lifetime.

IS HE A GONER?

"Fellas, you need to get here soon. The water is rising fast!" Several of the New Orleans police stations were not yet habitable. They had to combine several stations into one after Hurricane Katrina. The French Quarter was one of the areas not submerged by flood waters. All land lines were down. They had no cell phone service. Their only means of communication was one police radio station for the entire city.

An officer named Shorty was at the radio when the call came in. When the main levee could no longer hold back the flood waters, disaster engulfed New Orleans. One officer was at home. trying to figure out how he would get to the station. The flood waters were unstoppable. The officer radioed the police station. "Guys, I need to have a boat come pick me up … soon!!!"

When the other officers heard the drama unfolding, everyone but Shortly got off the air. The officer at home was backing up the stairs of his two-story home. Shorty implored him, "Can you swim out?"The officer at home responded, "I can't, Shorty. I'm not a good swimmer!"

The tension at the station was palpable. Shorty said, "Just hang on. We're trying to get a boat to you!"

"Shorty I'm up in my attic and the water is almost at my feet!"

Shorty tried desperately to talk him out. "Do you have a pipe or any way of punching a hole in the roof?"

"Hold on I'll look "was the frantic reply. The radio went silent for what seemed like an eternity. Then the radio sputtered,

"Nothing, I can't find anything!!"Some of the other officers wondered if it was too late, if they were about to lose a brother officer and friend.

Then Shorty had an idea. "Do you have your service belt on?"

The reply came back, "I do!"

Shorty knew the officers carried Glock pistols with 15 in the clip and 15 in their secondary clips.

"Can you shoot a hole in the roof?"

"Hold on, Shorty...I'll try!"

The radio went silent for what seemed like another eternity. No answer...no answer...no answer. Some thought it was all over. Hearts began to sink. No answer. Suddenly, the radio came alive.

"I'M OUT, I'M OUT! I'M ON THE ROOF!!"

The office went wild with cheers of joy and great relief. The officer was able to stay on his roof until help arrived.

This hair-raising account was told to my partner Pastor Randy Mantic and me by one of the brave officers present with Shorty in the temporary police station that day. We heard dozens of first-hand accounts during our two weeks in the Big Easy— New Orleans.

KIDS WERE SWEPT AWAY

The elementary school was full of students the morning the levee burst that terrible day in New Orleans. Water came rushing in like a murderous flood as teachers tried to get their students out of the classrooms and into the hallway to avoid impending disaster. It was too late.

A New Orleans Police officer stood at one end of the hallway as students were being washed past him as the water furiously rose. The officer was grabbing as many children as he could and placing them on the stairs behind him so they could scurry up to the second story of the school building, where they would be safe.

He saved many that day. Many washed past him and were swept away. One of the officers we walked with on Bourbon Street told partner Randy Mantik and me that the hero officer wasn't sleeping at night. He said all he could see were the faces of the children he couldn't reach. Children who were swept away, many of whom were never found.

That is the type of stress officers carried after Katrina. It is the kind of stress most of us can never understand.

THE PRACTICAL JOKER

It was eight weeks to the day when we arrived in New Orleans after Hurricane Katrina. I had handpicked nine therapists, hospital and police chaplains, and a real solid pastor. There were ten of us in all. We drove down to New Orleans in two cars and a semi-truck loaded with many thousands of dollars of medical equipment donated by Green Bay Aurora Baycare Hospital. As mentioned above, we went under the Franklin Graham disaster ministry Samaritan's Purse.

The city had not allowed anyone to do crisis counseling or debriefings of any kind before we got there. We stayed for just under two weeks. We organized our group into teams of two. My partner Pastor Randy Mantik and I were assigned the French Quarter police station, Number 8. We joined the officers for roll call at 5 p.m., then walked Bourbon Street until 1 or 2 in the morning.

What we saw, what we heard, what we still smelled after eight weeks was almost indescribable. The cops there hadn't had any more than a couple of days off that whole time. They worked 12-hour days. The stress levels were sometimes off the charts. They used cop humor to cope.

Here's one of the things they did to lighten up, even for a few moments. One officer, a 35-year-old named Bob, (I've changed the officers' names) had a truly wonderful knack for pulling practical jokes. He was brilliantly creative. Here's how one sergeant and one patrolman gave him some of his own medicine. Because they still couldn't get to the morgues, they had unfortunately lined up body bags next to the police station. The young officer, Sam, got into one of the body bags in the middle of several other full bags.

The sergeant zipped him inside and waited for Bob to come out. When he did, the sergeant asked him to pull each bag around the station to a shaded area. Bob did what he was asked. He slid several around the corner of the building, one at a time. Then he got to the one with a live body inside.

As soon as he started moving the bag with Sam inside, Sam sat up and screamed—loudly. He had scared the great practical joker out of his socks, Bob backed up four or five steps, pulled out his gun, and screamed, "DON'T YOU MOVE, MISTER!!!."

The sergeant quickly stepped between them. "Bob, don't shoot!" The great prankster was the honored victim of one of the greatest practical jokes I've ever heard.

When the young officer told Randy and me about this incredibly creative trick, the five or six officers who had been in the front area of the station—all of whom had probably heard the story at least ten times—laughed as uproariously as they had the first time they heard it.

JJ WATT

I enjoyed seeing football great JJ Watt as a CBS sportscaster today. Most of the people who watched him today probably aren't aware of what he did after the horrible murder of six people at the Christmas parade in Waukesha, Wisconsin.

My brother David's beautiful daughter Tammy was one of the victims that terrible day. Without any fanfare or sharing what he'd done, JJ quietly contacted all six families and told them he was going to pay the entire cost of the victims' funerals, just to be a quiet help in a very difficult time.

He and his family are from the Waukesha area. He also called my brother David a few days after the funeral to bring him comfort, and spent a half hour on the phone with him. This guy is a powerful example of a man caring for others, humbly and quietly.

I admire JJ greatly.

24 HOURS TO LIVE

The pain of a kidney stone is almost indescribable. Several nurses I've spoken with have told me it's worse than childbirth. I've never had a child but I've had five or six kidney stones and they are indeed miserable. The last one landed me at Aurora Baycare Medical Center here in Green Bay.

Marie was in the E.R. with me. They wheeled me out on my bed and took me to the C.T. scan room. It was an hour or two before they had the results of the scan. The doctor came into the room and told us that I indeed had several large kidney stones. Then he dropped a bomb. He told me that I also had four blood clots, one in each lung and one in each leg.

He looked me squarely in the eyes and said, "If we hadn't discovered this, you would have been dead by this time tomorrow." I almost felt the room shake like a California earthquake. The doc described the blood clots in my lungs as an inverted turkey wishbone, one end penetrating into each lung. I'd never had a blood clot before this.

In considering the cause, Marie and I came up with the probable answer. Somehow, we had failed to notice that one of my several medications, my blood thinner, had run out some time earlier. Kind of a big thing. But then we realized something even more important. If I hadn't had the terrible pain of the kidney stones, I never would have been in the hospital that day. The doctor said I had 24 hours to live. This is just one of several times that we know God surely intervened and saved my skin. He knew exactly how many hours I had left on my clock. 24.

THE HIGH DIVE

A 25-foot jump! That was the highest platform on the stationary wooden raft in West Bend, Wisconsin. The other two platforms, as memory serves me, were at 15 and 20 feet. The Milwaukee Police Annual Picnic was held there back in the 50s and 60s. I loved going with Mom and Dad and the other kids in our family. Brother David is a year older than me, but we could both swim at an early age. Even jumping from those stratospheric heights ... we were terrified and excited each time we jumped or dove.

Fast forward ten years. Best friend Scott Koval and I were heading back to Milwaukee from a camping trip. Our route took us right through West Bend and the public swimming lake I'd been to as a kid. We decided to spend the hot July afternoon at the park.

The first thing I did was swim out to the same old platform raft to challenge the terrifying top platform. Same raft. Same three tiers of terrifying platforms. I had to laugh out loud when I got to the three platforms. They were in order: 4 feet, 5 feet and 6 feet from the water.

Had they changed the raft and platforms? NO, not an inch. I'm no longer a scared eight-year-old. I'm 18 and a Milwaukee County lifeguard. It was all my PERCEPTION!! I had grown up. So, my point? Just wanted you to look at some of the very scary things you are facing today. Are you looking through a child's eyes? Or, are you looking through the eyes of someone Christ changed—from childish fear to confident man or woman who has learned to trust God to make the scary things conquerable. Make the 25-foot platform a 5-foot hop. Fear has a way of making things seem worse than they really are. Are you fearful of things God wants to come alongside you and whisper: "I've got this, son. I'm here."

STRANGE NEW WORLD

Seems we're not alone. My brother David stopped for lunch at Waukesha Memorial Hospital recently. He got into a conversation with a friendly female cafeteria employee. She explained that she was working there just to help supplement her day job income. Seems the economy has affected her just like the rest of us. Her day job? She's a medical doctor there at Waukesha Memorial Hospital. Strange new world......

THE TRUTH OF THE REDWOODS

Hiking in one of California's giant redwood groves some years back, we were joined by a very knowledgeable park ranger. On one particular trail, we walked beneath a huge redwood on the hillside above us. Fully one third of its roots were open and exposed.

Someone asked how such a massive (heavy) redwood could continue to remain upright. His answer surprised and stuck with me. He explained that in spite of their incredible size, redwoods have a very shallow root system. Even though some of those trees date back to Christ's time, they haven't been toppled by earthquakes, gale-force winds, or even forest fires.

Their secret? Their root systems are shallow but extremely far-reaching. Their strength comes from intertwining with other redwoods' roots. Simply, they hold each other up. That's why you'll never find a lone redwood. It lacks the strength of unity.

It's interesting to me that we humans (who are supposed to be vastly more intelligent than redwoods) often fail to incorporate that profound truth. WE NEED EACH OTHER!!! We hold each other up!

This is just a reminder to all of you whom I love. Don't be an island. I'm speaking this to myself first—I can't go it alone. Did I hear someone say "Amen?"

THE SENTENCE:
OVERWHELMING PRAISE

True story. I shared this in a sermon a few years back. There is a village in Africa that has a crime rate that is right near zero. Crime of any kind. Here's what they do.

When a person of any age is found to have committed a crime of any level, they don't bring jail time or even a court proceeding. Instead, they have the person sit on a chair in the middle of the public area. Then, one by one, every person in the village, young and old, stands in front of the offender and declares everything they love or appreciate about that person. Sometimes this process takes a day or more.

By the time they all shower the person with overwhelming love, the person loses the desire to offend ANYBODY! Peace and tranquility continue.

We all know someone who feels they have wronged someone. Maybe it's YOU they've wronged. Anger and unforgiveness rarely solve anything. Who needs a word of forgiveness, compassion, encouragement?

Consider the tribe in Africa.

THE NEW WORLD OF AIDS

What do I do? It was all new to us. The horrible AIDS epidemic was sweeping across America and across much of the world. We had to write manuals for church volunteers and staff to explain how we were to keep people (especially children) safe.

In those first couple of years in the early 1980s, nobody seemed to know for sure how the deadly disease spread. Casual contact? Bodily fluids? Breathing? It was a very existential issue that everyone was taking very seriously!

One day, I got a visit in my office. It was Dianna Cadiente, our very talented music and worship leader.

"Dan," she started. "I have a really big favor to ask." She explained that a woman who worked at her mom's beauty shop was desperately trying to find someone willing to visit her dying son on his sick bed. He was growing weaker by the hour. AIDS was killing him.

My first reaction was to agree right away, but suddenly, the doubts and fears jumped in. Nobody knew if it could be transmitted through a handshake, a hug, a breath. I thought about those things for several moments before I answered her. "Sure, I'll go. Do you have his address?" I went the following day, rang the doorbell and a very frail voice invited me in.

What do I do? How do I possibly greet him? "God, he belongs to you and I belong to you. Give me wisdom and protection, Father." He had been an athlete and a seasoned sailor. A photo on the TV showed him with his beautiful sailing yacht. I reached out my hand and he reached out as well. He held onto my hand

and looked at me with some fear and nervousness. I sensed he wanted me to just hold him for a moment. I did.

The nervousness seemed to just leave the room. We spoke openly and honestly for an hour or so. He'd lived a very successful and interesting life. But he wanted to talk about God. He knew his days were very limited. I shared God's plan of salvation and he listened very attentively. That afternoon, he willingly opened his heart and received Christ as Savior. I met with him a week later. He was more frail than before, now down to 120 pounds from 190.

He wanted me to understand his funeral wishes clearly. "Preach Jesus!" He wanted his family and friends to hear the gospel as he had. A week later he was gone. We held his funeral right on one of the Santa Cruz beaches, just feet from the ocean he loved. I'd embraced him several times in my visits. God touched him and protected me. It was one of those encounters I'll never forget.

THE GREAT JOHNNY BENCH

What a bomb!! Pastor Ray Shelton and I were enjoying a beautiful Saturday at Pebble Beach Country Club in Carmel CA. It was the AT&T PRO AM 3rd day of competition. We watched as some of the world's greatest golfers, both professional and amateur, put on an incredible display. We were standing at the dogleg 15th (if memory serves me) at about 300 yards from the tee. We watched shot after shot fall near where we were standing.

Golfers included actor Don Johnson, Vice President Dan Quayle, and the amateur with the biggest crowd following him all day, football great Joe Montana. Dan Quayle had three body-guards. Joe Montana had six!!!

Suddenly, one golf ball went flying 30 or 40 yards past every golfer, both pro and amateur. The crowd let out a loud OOOOOOOH!! Who in the world had that much power in his swing? Tiger Woods? John Daly? I asked out loud, "Who in the world was that!!!???"

A man standing next to me had the day's lineup. He got a big grin on his face as he read off the golfer's name. "That was Johnny Bench!!"It immediately made sense to those of us old enough to remember the incredible career of the Cincinnati Reds' all-star catcher. As he walked past us, a huge roar went up from the crowd. I noticed that his wrists were about the size of most men's biceps.

It was a day I'll never forget. Just a few feet from a living legend. It was a VERY good day....

THE FOLDED NAPKIN

It's just a few more weeks until Easter. I'd like to plant a great promise that many people, especially westerners, overlook. It's found in John 20:6+7...

When the disciples heard that the tomb was empty, Peter and John got up and ran to the tomb. John arrived first, looked in and saw that Christ was indeed gone. Peter passed John into the tomb and saw the grave cloths lying there on the slab where Jesus had been laid. But the part I want to look at is the napkin that they had placed on Jesus' face. The grave clothes were lying there in no particular order.

John took care to remember the position of the napkin. It was not just left behind in a particular pattern. It was folded neatly and set apart from the other grave cloths. That doesn't mean a whole lot to those of us in 21st century America. But it was a very important message to those in Israel 2,100 years ago.

Every servant would know the message of the folded napkin. If the master of the household wanted the servants to know that he was finished eating, he would leave his napkin next to his plate unfolded. But every servant knew that if the master left his napkin folded next to his plate, it meant he was leaving but returning shortly to the table. The servants would remain at the table ready for the master's return.

The message Jesus left to the disciples and all of us we dare not miss. Jesus is saying to all of us this Easter season, "I have left you for a while but I am returning soon!!"Think about that as we come into this very special time of year called Easter!!

THE COCKCROW

Just an Easter lesson for my family and friends. Luke records Peter's denial of Christ the day Christ was brutally beaten then crucified. (22:54-62) Most in the West are not aware of what the Bible calls "the cockcrow" referred to. Truly, it had nothing to do with a rooster or any other animal.

The "cockcrow" was a shofar horn blast heard from the Jerusalem wall every night at 9pm, 12am, and 3am telling the city "all is well...no enemies approaching." Luke says that at the 2nd cockcrow (midnight) Peter heard that "all is well" trumpet blast. All was not well for Peter!! He felt all was lost and he'd denied the Messiah he swore he'd never deny. He heaved wave after wave of remorseful tears.

The cockcrow was his undoing that night. He thought "all is lost...I'm the worst of the worst!!"Poor Peter....but then.... Easter Sunday came!!! HE IS RISEN!!!! Tell me, every time Peter heard the cockcrow after that day...was he reminded of his own failure on Good Friday, or Christ's victory Easter morning? My guess— all he remembered was: HE IS RISEN!!!! What day will WE focus on?

I DIDN'T COME TO TAKE SIDES!!

Joshua just didn't get it. God had given Israel victory after victory....including separating the Red Sea to save their lives from slaughter by Pharaoh's army. God was about to give them another huge victory: the fertile land of Jericho as their possession.

Joshua was alone when a powerful warrior with a razor-sharp sword stood in front of him. Joshua knew immediately that this was no ordinary soldier. But his response in Joshua 5 was so much like our responses when we pray for—anything.

I'll paraphrase: Joshua asked, "Alright sir, I just want to know one thing....are you on OUR SIDE or are you on THEIR SIDE?" The great soldier, whom we believe was Christ incarnate, gave him an answer I just love.

Again, I paraphrase: "Am I on YOUR SIDE or on THEIR SIDE???!!!! Joshua, you just don't get it yet. I didn't come here to take sides....I came to TAKE OVER!!!"Joshua kneeled in humble submission.

Friends, so often when we pray, we want to know..."God, are you on MY SIDE?? God, will you give me what I'm praying for?" And God is still saying today: "I didn't come to take YOUR SIDE....I CAME TO TAKE OVER!!"

I think so often we miss it when we pray. Do we miss God like Joshua did long ago? God wants to know just one thing from us. "Are you on MY SIDE? Are you surrendering your will to MY WILL?"Please keep this in mind today as you pray.

ANGRY YOUNG MAN

He said he was a student at the University of Wisconsin-Green Bay. He was visiting Woodland Worship Center on Hwy. 172, 1½ miles west of the airport for the first time that Sunday morning. I had spoken about the incredible grace of God demonstrated in the death of Christ.

After the service, he came up to me in the foyer and introduced himself. He said he had some questions about my message. After speaking with him for a couple of minutes, it became clear that he was in some pretty strong disagreement with what I'd said that morning. His teaching as he grew up was that salvation was a joint effort, God did some things but we had to do our part in the process by performing enough good works to be acceptable to Him.

Without coming on too strong, I tried to establish what the Bible says is crystal clear. "We are saved by grace through faith, not of works lest any man should boast." (Ephesians 2:8+9) As much as I tried to converse calmly with this very bright young man, I could tell he was becoming more and more agitated.

After several minutes of trying to reason with him, he seemed to reach a boiling point. He blurted out, "You make it sound like GOD DID THE WHOLE THING!!"

My answer was really just one word..."Bingo!!"

He just wasn't having any of it. He was convinced that salvation was God strictly doing His work and us doing certain works for true salvation. I was not able to penetrate his sad theology. We said our goodbyes and he left in a huff, never to return.

I wondered how many thousands (millions?) are bound in such an impossible doctrine. Friends, He did it ALL and when the incredible sacrifice was made, He said three wonderful words.... "IT IS FINISHED!!!"

STRATEGY?
YEAH, I'M GOING TO BEAT HIM

Our son Ben was 12 or 13 and about to compete in one of his last Tae Kwon Do tournaments. It happened to be held in Green Bay that year, at Ben's own middle school, Benjamin Franklin. By this point in his life, he would be Wisconsin state champion, twice, and ranked number seven in the U.S. Junior Olympics. In other words, he was ranked number seven in the nation.

He'd already competed in the board-breaking (¾-inch pine). He was the only kid to break more than one thickness. He broke two with a flying side-kick. He shattered the two boards and won his second gold medal that day.

Now the final and toughest competition: sparring. The participants wear protection on their heads, chest and torso area, hands and forearms, and thigh protection. I was sitting on a bleacher near the final competitions and observing the kid Ben would fight. He looked tough.

I called Ben down from the top bleacher where he was waiting and just hanging out with a buddy. I saw other parents talking strategy with their kids, getting them as ready as possible. "I'm not being a very good dad," I reasoned. So, I called him down and said, "Hey, bud... this kid looks pretty tough. Do you have a strategy worked out?"

And as only Ben could answer, without a bit of bragging, "Yeah....I'm going to beat him."

Solomon said it in Proverbs 23:7, "As a man thinks in his heart, SO IS HE!!"Can you guess what happened? Of course, Ben whooped him and won his third gold medal that day. Again, ranked #1 in Wisconsin.

Q: What do you think about YOU??? How do you see yourself in your heart of hearts? What you see in yourself is without a doubt the way you will live, think, respond.

For Ben, there was ZERO OPTION FOR ANYTHING ELSE!!! Consider this today, won't you?

SLAPPED SILLY!

I just didn't think before I acted. I was in our living room at our home on 73rd and Van Beck in Milwaukee. Five of my friends and I were "slap-boxing." We would play fight two at a time, using an open palm rather than a closed fist. It was about two steps down from real boxing or MMA, although we didn't pull our slaps and sometimes we'd come out with bright red cheeks from getting pummeled.

On this day, slap boxing took on a new meaning. We'd been sparring for a half hour or so when my dad walked through the living room. "Hey, Carlson, slap-box with your dad."

So, I said, "Dad, how about one round?"

My friends were egging me on. I thought I was tough as nails and their challenging words gave me real bravado. My dad was facing me when I made my first mistake. I couldn't resist. I popped him on his left cheek...not real hard but not a love tap either.

"Danny...no." My friends continued goading me.

Then I made a really BAD decision. I reached out and gave my dad another pop on the right cheek, harder than the first one. Those of you who knew my tough police sergeant dad are probably thinking, "Dan, did you LOSE YOUR MIND????"

Well, the next thing I knew, I had traveled from the middle of the room to flat against the wall with my head flying from left to right to left. You get the picture. I'd become a human punching bag, and he wasn't pulling his slaps!! The encounter probably only lasted 10 or 15 seconds, but long enough for him to bop me 25 or 30 times. My friends were rolling on the carpet in hysterics.

Sarge asked, "Do you want to keep going, Danny?"

"No sir, no sir, no sir!!!"

My friends thought it was a really entertaining match. I, on the other hand, did not. I never challenged my dad again.

SHAME IS DEADLY!

A number of years ago, a man named Sir Francis Conan Doyle decided to play a trick on five of his friends. He sent a telegram that said, "All is known. Flee!!"Not one, not two, but all five immediately left England and fled to France. For different reasons, shame was eating away at all five.

Shame is different than guilt. Guilt can be helpful in convincing us to change our behavior. We've all felt it, some of us more than once. But shame is never healthy.

Guilt says, "I did something wrong."

Shame says, "I AM WRONG." It is insidious and always harmful. It goes much, much deeper than guilt and often makes us think that even God can't help this. Behavior experts say that it typically takes about three days to slide from guilt, (which was intended to turn us around and make things right) to shame, an emotional cancer God never intended for us to carry.

Shame is DEADLY!! It condemns us. John 3:17 declares, "For God did NOT come into the world to condemn the world, but that the world through Him might be saved."

Are you feeling guilty about something you've done? Take it to the cross where Jesus carried it away. Then, LEAVE IT AT THE CROSS!! It has been paid for!!

But if you are feeling shame, you MUST stop living under that crushing weight. Stop living a life based on your feelings (which can and do lie to us) and determine to live a life based on God's Word, which never lies and is always healthy!!

GUILT can be healthy in directing us to the cross. SHAME? Is never healthy and always destructive. You are not equipped to live under its horrible, crushing weight. Remember what Jesus said on the cross? IT IS FINISHED!!!

SAMPSON THE AVERAGE GUY

If I asked you to describe Sampson in the Old Testament Book of Judges, how would you describe him? The movie industry shows him looking like Arnold Schwarzenegger or The Rock, huge with muscles, and a great heartthrob for the ladies. A big powerful beast of a man, a man many boys wish they were like.

Is that more or less your concept of Sampson? If it is, you'd be absolutely wrong!! Remember Delilah? Again, and again she tried to trick him. In Judges 16:6, some men had offered her a huge sum of money. Here's what she did: "And Delilah said to Sampson, tell me the secret of your great strength." These men were Philistines and had a great hatred toward Sampson. He'd killed some of them and embarrassed all of them.

Finally, he gave into her constant badgering and told her the secret. But even Sampson hadn't figured this one out. It wasn't his muscles because he appeared just like other men around him. It wasn't even in his goldilocks hair. No, his strength came from just one source—God. If God had made him a big muscle man, everyone would have thought that that was his secret.

NO, God was the ONLY SOURCE OF HIS INCREDIBLE ABILITY. I don't know about you, but I need His strength to make it through every day! Whose strength have you been relying on lately? I mean REALLY RELYING ON?

Maybe this little true story will get you to refocus your focus. Get your focus on Him and do your best to keep it on Him. Hopefully, this will help some of you.

PET PEEVES

Just in case you weren't sure, it is "nu-clear," not "nu-cu-lar." It is "converse," not "conversate." For wonderful Wisconsin treasures, it is "boat," not "bo-aht." It is "No," not "no-ah." It is "you," not "youse." It is "we were," not "we was."

It is "Mil-wau-kee," not M'waukee." It is "I just saw," not "I just seen." It is "the Bears," not "da Bears—wait, it IS da Bears. It is "bubbler," not "water fountain."

It is "land of 15,000 lakes"—Wisconsin really DOES have 5,000 more lakes than Minnesota. (We just don't brag about it.)

It is "wash," not "worsh." It is "Milwaukee Braves" not "Atlanta Braves" (Are any of you still heartbroken they left? I guess I'm probably holding onto that one too long.)

It is "a long way," not "a long ways." It is "surrounded," not completely surrounded" (Surrounded means surrounded.)

It is "take it home with you," not "bring it home with you."

It is water heater, not hot water heater—you don't need to heat water that's already heated. Come on, man!!!

It's "the land of the free and the home of the brave" and that, dear friends, will NEVER change.

ORGANISM!

You can't back up the clock. That's what I wanted to do. It was 28 years ago and I was the associate pastor at the great Milwaukee central city church Parklawn Assembly of God. I was teaching an adult Sunday school class of about 50. The class was flowing really nicely with good discussion and attention. I was teaching on the church as a united body, each member doing his/her part to strengthen and build up the body of Christ.

There was a point during the class that I wanted to make a special point about the power of unity. My voice got a little louder as I planted this Bible truth to each one. I declared, "The body truly functions as an organism." It got really quiet and in just a moment, I realized that I hadn't said the word, "organism," but said a word very close to that.

One person in back couldn't help laughing, then another and another. You get the picture. All I could do was say the word I was trying to say...."organism!!"By this time, the entire class was in hysterics. My face was five shades of red. I couldn't see it but I could surely feel it. By now class time was about over. I finished with these words, "I'll never gain control of this class again!!"Again, uproarious laughter.

Don't you know, they had some hilarious conversations later at home over lunch.

MARIE'S ENTERTAINMENT

I'm my wife Marie's favorite entertainment. I make her laugh even when I'm not trying to. She was almost in hysterics a couple of weeks ago when I took a nose dive.

It wasn't when it happened, but rather an hour or two later in the hospital. I've been losing weight at a pretty good clip—that's with the wonderful thing called a catheter and water pills.

Plus, I've been very careful with my diet. Since the first of September, I've lost 65 pounds. That's a bunch. And if you combine that with chemicals like electrolytes being out of balance, getting light-headed is not uncommon.

So, I was in the bathroom about to weigh myself when I got extremely dizzy, passed out, smacking my nose on the window sill and went down hard on the floor. The bridge of my nose was pouring out blood. My right nostril flowed like a river and left the bathroom floor looking like a gruesome crime scene.

The ambulance came and took me to the Aurora ER. It was there that Marie just split a gut laughing at what I said. It sounds silly now but I asked her if my hair was really messed up.

I couldn't see at first what was so funny.

She said, "Honey, your face is covered with blood. You look like a Halloween mask—and you're worried about your hair being out of place!!!??"

I finally saw what she was talking about when I took my cell phone and pointed the camera at myself like a mirror. Yikes!!! I scared MYSELF!! No, Marie isn't a cold-hearted meany. She just has a crazy husband who makes her laugh (whether I'm trying to or not).

MILWAUKEE'S DUMBEST CRIMINAL

Criminals truly are not known to be terribly bright. Best buddy Scott Koval, a retired Greenfield police lieutenant, shared this true account:

Armed bad guy gets stopped for a traffic violation near 76th and Grange in Greendale. Bad guy runs into a wooded area. Police set up a perimeter and bad guy was soon found and arrested, but not until he had time to ditch his pistol. A Belgian Malinois police dog (sometimes called a German Shepherd on crack) was called in to sniff out the pistol, which he quickly did.

At the station, the bad guy tried to deny ever having the gun. Enter very large police dog. The cops told the not-so-bright-guy that the dog was able to tell them whether the gun belonged to him or not, simply by smell. "Hold very still. The dog will tell us if this is your gun." In Dutch, the dog handler instructed the very bright K9 to smell both bad guy and pistol. He followed orders perfectly. Then the dog was instructed to sit.

"Does this gun belong to this man?" Of course, the dog wasn't able to do this, but at the command, the dog barked once. "Yes, this is the guy's gun" the training officer interpreted for the pup.

"OK, sir, Does the gun belong to you?"

Not-so-smart's answer. "Well, of course it's my gun. The dog just told you, didn't he??!!"

Case closed. Bad guy found Guilty!!!!

Hmmmmm....guilty of the illegal possession or guilty of being a moron?? You decide.

IT MAKES ME WANT TO DANCE!

Dr. C.M. Ward was one of, the most prolific and powerful speakers I've ever heard. He was also president of Bethany Bible College in Santa Cruz, CA. when I attended there way back in the 70s. He was about to preach to the 700 or so students during chapel.

On this particular weekday morning, a gifted musical group began the worship time. I don't remember their name or where they were from. What I do remember is how lively and LOUD their music was. The students were lifted up in worship and praise. It was truly a chapel time I'll never forget.

I was sitting about half way back in the sanctuary, trying my best to see Dr. Ward's reaction to this exciting gospel group, but students were all on their feet blocking him from my sight. He was already in his late 70s and moved slowly as he walked.

The music group sat down as the great preacher slowly climbed the five or six steps up to platform level. I could hardly contain my anticipation. What would he say? How would he react to this LOUD and lively worship group?

He went slowly to the podium, every eye fixed on him. Then he spoke in that gravely, unmistakable voice. Here's what he said. "Do you want to know how I feel about this music?" After a pregnant pause, he continued..."It makes me wanna DANCE!!"

The students went crazy for about 30 seconds, voicing their resounding approval. Friends, I'd like to invite you to join me in 2024. I want life to make me wanna dance. I'm going to do all that God wants me to be, all He wants me to do. And giving all, I have to allow God to have all He wants of my life. I'm already laying the track to move forward in His will, plan and purpose.

Here's a part of His plan...as of three months ago, I'd lost 75 pounds, I've been exercising regularly, and I'm determined that I'm going to let God be my dance partner. I want ALL He has in store for me.

Will you join me? There's no pressure, no counting on some-one else to help make you want to dance through the year 2024. How do you REALLY feel about the next 365 days? Give me a text and let me know if you'd like to join me. Have a blessed New Year,

IMMENSE EMBARRASSMENT!

I was scheduled to preach that Sunday morning at Parklawn Assembly of God on the north side of Milwaukee. It was a very warm summer day and just an hour before the service, one of the ushers told me that the fairly old air conditioner had stopped working. Only a few of us knew where the reset mechanism was.

I hurried to the narrow, dark, equipment room. The morning would have been very uncomfortable without A/C. The sanctuary seats close to 1,500 and is usually quite full. That many people produce considerable heat.

The pressure of making sure the unit would function properly was tangible. The reset switch was just two feet off the cement floor and the lighting was poor at best. As I bent down to flip the switch, the unthinkable happened. The room had mechanisms on both sides of the narrow aisle.

I flipped the switch and I heard a very clear *rrrip*. A sharp piece of metal behind me had torn a perfect four-inch L-shaped tear in my best suit pants, right at the base of my back right pocket. I was mortified! I knew that the choir would be sitting behind me the entire service. Embarrassing!!!

I had no choice but to call out to God and ask Him to PLEASE help me get through that sermon. Straight away, I felt calm and I was able to preach my message fairly well. As all the pastors at Parklawn did at the end of every sermon, I gave an altar call, just hoping someone would have the message penetrate their heart. Here again I silently prayed for God's Spirit to take over.

Remarkably, about 22 people got out of their seats and made their way to the altar to receive Christ as Savior. Two hours earlier, I hadn't been sure I'd be able to focus on what I was to do. Friends, I was UTTERLY depending on God to get me through an otherwise very embarrassing situation.

Bottom line—that's all He EVER wants of us. To rely solely on Him to see us through every situation.

Question: what is your situation right now...today?

GIVE ME ST. LOUIS!

This is a personal story that took place about 35 years ago after the birth of our son Ben. Marie had had some fairly severe complications with her blood sugar going dangerously high before and during Ben's birth. Thank God, both mother and baby came through with flying colors.

A short time later, Marie and I decided that Ben would be our third and final child. I volunteered to be the one who would undergo the minor surgery to prevent another pregnancy.

I was pastoring in Rice Lake, Wisconsin at the time. There was one hospital in town and I visited church members there fairly often. As I thought about the procedure I would undergo, I felt I really wanted to have it done fairly far away from the town, just to save myself the embarrassment of a nurse who would recognize me while doing the prep work. You guys who have had this done know exactly what I'm talking about.

I came up with a solution that I thought would be safe. I got in contact with a doctor all the way down in Eau Claire, some 60 miles south, to do the minor surgery. On the appointed day, I made the one-hour drive, fully assured that nobody would know who I was and saving me embarrassment.

I was taken into one of the procedure rooms, where I was placed on an examination table and waited there 15 minutes or so. I was comfortable and at ease knowing this would be a brief and fairly painless procedure and I wouldn't need to see people I saw on a regular basis. So far, so good.

When the door opened, a very friendly nurse came in, took one look at me and said, "Pastor Dan, how wonderful to see you here!!" *Aaaarg!!!!*

I immediately thought I should have made the appointment in St. Louis!

BE GRATEFUL, DAN

I was heading north on Hwy.17 from Santa Cruz to Bethany Bible College in Scott's Valley, California, a 15-minute drive into the beautiful Santa Cruz mountains. Marie and I owned a sky-blue Ford Grenada, a nice car for college students back then. We felt blessed because it was really nicer than some of the cars owned by the professors then, mostly because the cost of housing was and is astronomical in that area.

I had to chuckle at myself on this particular school day. I was in the left lane and something caught my eye in the right lane. It was a beautiful gray Mercedes just ahead of me, so I got a really good look at it. I remember thinking, "Oooh, I'd really love to have that beauty."

Then I saw something that made me grin. The guy in the Mercedes was eyeballing the car directly ahead of me. It was a gorgeous silver Rolls Royce and the Mercedes guy was locked in staring at it.

How ironic, I thought. "I want something better, more comfortable, better looking. Mercedes guy was thinking the same thing. Wanting something bigger, better, more beautiful, more prestigious. Reality got ahold of me.

"Lord, I don't need a Rolls Royce. I don't need a Mercedes. I really like the car you've blessed us with. Lord, from the bottom of my heart, thank You for blessing us!!"

This Thanksgiving, remember to keep things in perspective. Give Him thanks for all He's done for you and all the blessings He's lovingly showered you with. Happy Thanksgiving to all of you!!!

A FISHING FOOL

Father's Day brought back a not-so-funny incident that happened in my office in Rice Lake. A man I'd never met before called, then came by. "Pastor, I really need help. My wife said she's going to leave me."

"Why don't you tell me what's going on?"

"Well, I guess it may have something to do with my fishing."

He went on to say, "When I get off of work, I usually spend some time in my boat just to relax."

I wanted to hear more. "So, what time do you usually get home?"

"Well, it's usually 9 or 10 o'clock"

Now he's really got my interest. I asked if they had any kids.

He looked a little sheepish. "Yeah, we have four.""

"OK ... do you help put the kids to bed?"

Another sheepish look. "Well, not really. My wife has already fed them, given them baths, and put them to bed."

I had to find out. "How often do you go fishing?"

His answer floored me. "Usually six times."

"A month?"

Now he looked really sheepish. "No, that's each week, but Pastor, I don't want to lose her!!"

It was all I could do to not say, "Are you kidding me!!!??"After further discussion, I had to get to the elephant in the room.

"Are you really serious about keeping her?"

"Yeah, I'm really serious!!!"

I always try to get couples to compromise. "Well, to start with, would you begin by going right home from work, at least some of the time?" You wouldn't believe the look of pain on his face.

He didn't say anything for some time. I thought he'd agree to at least some days. But he didn't. He wouldn't. I told him I thought a divorce was almost certain. His countenance was despair and sadness. He wouldn't budge.

I shook his hand, wished him well and said goodbye. Happy ending? Sorry, I knew they couldn't last and divorced shortly later.

Fellas, this is a true account of our discussion that day. Let me just remind all of us to keep our priorities straight. Personally, I have to do this often. Let the main thing be the main thing!!

Can I get an Amen?

A MILWAUKEE HERO

It was freezing cold in Milwaukee that February night. It was years ago when cops walked the beat in the downtown area. Some of you remember the police call boxes with the blue light on top. When the light flashed, they would unlock the door and answer the call from number one precinct.

Two young officers ran to the box when they saw the light that cold winter night. Bernie and Jim got the call, "Man in the river next to Riverside Theater." Immediately, they ran around the back of the Riverside. They knew there was a metal ladder on the wall going right down to water level there.

Jim was a better swimmer. He quickly took off his shoes, gun belt, and heavy winter coat. He climbed down the ladder and without hesitation, jumped into the freezing water. He had to swim around huge chunks of ice to get to the man they later learned was trying to commit suicide.

When his lungs felt the freezing water, he immediately lost his breath. He treaded water until he could breathe again. He saw a large plank floating nearby. He grabbed it and swam to the drowning man. By this time, the guy had changed his mind about suicide. Now, all he could think of was staying alive. Jim got to him in just minutes. He pulled the poor guy onto the plank and began the freezing swim back to Bernie.

By this time, the fire department was on scene and together, they got the guy out. Thank God, the man got help for his depression and lived many more years.

Jim and Bernie both received letters of commendation and Jim received the Medal of Honor from the police department. At the time, he was the only living officer to earn the medal. Most were given posthumously. Jim was truly a humble man. He never spoke of that freezing Milwaukee winter night.

My brother David and I were going through our dad's scrapbook one afternoon. That's the first time we'd heard about this heroic cop's swim on a freezing February night. He told us about the guy living a good many years after a young beat cop pulled him out and saved his life.

Suffice it to say, Dave and Dan Carlson were awesomely proud of our dad, Sergeant Jim Carlson.

DAVID DUPLISEIS

Some of you old-timers may remember the name David Du-Pliseis? He was small in stature, 5'6"or so and maybe 140lbs. He had gone around the world preaching the gospel for decades when I first heard him. Much of his ministry was done in Africa, sometimes miles away from paved roads or electricity. But he preached with such authority that many entire villages became Christians.

David's nickname was Mr. Pentecost. It's been 45 years since I heard him preach in Santa Cruz, California. His stories of great conversions were powerful and exciting. One thing he said that Sunday morning had little to do with missionary work. It dealt with people who came to him asking if he would PLEASE help them with their marriages, many of which were on the brink of failure.

I'll never forget the advice he gave to the hundreds who came to him over the years. Here's the foolproof truth he gave to every couple: "GET THE SIN OUT OF YOUR LIVES AND YOU ARE GUARANTEED A SUCCESSFUL MARRIAGE."

A number of people laughed that day, but he wasn't fooling. It's been 45 years since I heard him speak, and that advice has never escaped my mind. This giant of faith has long since left this world, but his words and his legacy will live forever. *Selah.*

HE SAVED 67 CENTS!

I had the perfect job during college years. I was a dispatcher for 3A Emergency Road Service in Santa Cruz, California. It paid well and allowed me to attend class during the day. Because Santa Cruz is a beach town surrounded by the gorgeous Santa Cruz mountains, we heard some crazy stories from the tow truck drivers.

Hwy. 17 is the main 4-lane highway between the South Bay (Silicone Valley) and the beach. It is both steep and winding. A tow truck driver stopped by our 3A office after his call and told me the story.

Heading south toward Santa Cruz, a not-so-brainiac had an ingenious idea. Driving his friend's new Mercedes, he decided to save a few cents on gas. At the summit, he put the car in neutral, turned off the very expensive Mercedes, and began the 6-mile winding, coasting descent.

Great idea??? Well, it would have been if the STEERING WHEEL HADN'T LOCKED!! By the time the frantic driver figured out what he'd done, the car was off the highway plummeting 120 feet down the mountainside.

The cheapskate driver lived; the car did not. But he saved 67 cents on gas!!! Imagine facing his friend to explain the terrible crash. Do you think he finished the story with, "Oh, but I saved 67 cents on gas?"

UNWORTHY MR. CAMPOLO!!

Let me share an account of Christian author and speaker, Tony Campolo. Tony has spoken to tens of thousands of college and high-school students over the years. Here's the story:

During his years at seminary, he had a professor who was exceptionally brilliant and a powerful Bible theologian. He said this man was admired by faculty and students alike. One day, as the class was starting, the professor asked Tony to begin the class with prayer. Tony said his heart was in his throat. He didn't want to embarrass himself before this professor and began his prayer with these words: "Dear Father, please hear the prayer of a worthless sinner ..."

He was mortified when the professor interrupted him in not a small voice. "NO, Mr. Campolo, unworthy not worthless. Continue. "

Tony doesn't remember what he prayed after that powerful and profound interruption. But he never forgot that five-second interruption. We were ALL unworthy. But to God we are made perfectly acceptable in Christ Jesus. (Romans 5:1)

I heard Tony Campolo share this story about 35 years ago, and just as he never forgot his great professor's words, I have never forgotten Tony's great insight into God. Maybe someone could use this reminder today. God bless you all!!

THE POWER OF THE WAVES

"My people perish for lack of knowledge." (Hosea 4:6)

It was one of Israel's darkest times. The northern and southern kingdoms were at heated odds against each other. Jerusalem and the southern kingdom were so angry and defiant with the northern kingdom that they sought help from the dreaded Assyrians to fight the north.

The people had turned their backs on God to worship pagan idols. The prophet Hosea saw the terrible place God's people had slipped into, and so he cried out God's warning.

Now, let me jump ahead 2,740 years, to the end of 2023. I've watched with great interest the massive storm hitting the California coast. Twenty- to forty-foot-high waves are slamming the coast between San Francisco and Big Sur, with the town of Santa Cruz directly in the bullseye.

Marie and I lived just six blocks from the beach and West Cliff Dr. In Santa Cruz, people ignorant of the power and patterns of waves would stand too close to the edge of the cliffs, placing them in deadly danger. They are not aware of "sets"...the way waves will come in in smaller size. Then, without warning, a couple of much larger waves come crashing in, sweeping in over their heads, dragging them off the cliffs and against the rock walls below.

Every year, several people with a LACK OF KNOWLEDGE of waves, some in critical shape, some dead, are taken to local hospitals. This week, deadly waves many times larger than typical wave sets are dragging people to their deaths. Police and lifeguards try to warn people to stay well back of the cliffsides. Many think they can outwit or outrun these water mountains. I've found myself wanting to holler at the TV, "Get back you knuckleheads. You are about to die without warning."

In 2024, what things does God want you to have knowledge of? Is He speaking to you about an important issue you'll need to have knowledge of? Are you listening? *Selah* (think about these things) and have a great and blessed New Year!! Dan

THE AGAPE FORCE

They were called the Agape Force. They were a group of young adults from around the U.S. and were very active during the 1970s and '80s in California and other parts of the country.

One of the key leaders many of you will remember. His name was Barry McGuire, the pop musician who wrote and sang the song *Eve of Destruction*. He'd become a committed Christian and was very active in forming and leading the Agape Force. Several hundred young adults were part of this Christian outreach group. They traveled around California mostly but also to other parts of the country. We got to know them in the town of Los Banos, where Marie and I were married. We worked with them on a number of occasions to reach people for Christ.

They had some very interesting rules for ministry. One of those rules was followed during meal times. They had rented two houses. The men stayed in one, the women in the other. The men's house was larger and had a very long dining room table that would seat about 20. Marie and I shared a number of meals there with them.

One of the rules struck a chord with me and I've remembered it ever since. The rule was, if you wanted anything passed to you, you could never ask for it. If you wanted more meat or potatoes or milk, you could not ask. The way food was passed was somebody ELSE had to notice that there was something missing on your plate or in your cup. They would ask if you would like them to pass it to you. This forced people to be always aware of the needs of others around the table. I thought it was a great way to live a

Christian life—always being aware of the needs of others. Because they had such servant's hearts, God was able to use the Agape Force to reach thousands for His kingdom. Wonder whose needs God wants me/you to notice today.

WE EIGHT KINGS

We all know the verses...Matthew 2:1-12, speaking of the kings or wise men visiting the Christ child. They bore gifts; we know that. The gifts were precious commodities—gold, frankincense, and myrrh; we know that. They followed a brilliant star to the King of Kings; we know that.

But here's something I'd guess you didn't know. Here it is: there were actually eight wise men, or was it eleven? Maybe it was nine or four.

Dan, EVERYONE knows there were three. After all, we sing it every Christmas time. *We Three Kings of Orient Are*. We know the three types of gifts presented.

But where does it say that only one king brought only one gift each? Or, did four kings bring gold, three bring frankincense, and one bring myrrh? You say that's ridiculous, Dan.

Oh, yeah...? Prove it. Why even challenge such a time-honored tradition? Here's why. And it's simple. When you read God's Word, be VERY CAREFUL to never add anything or subtract anything of your own doing. How many really believe the Bible says, "Cleanliness is next to godliness?" It never says that. Nor does it say, "God will never give you more than you can handle." Anywhere!!!

What it DOES say is that God will never allow you to be tempted beyond which He will give you a means of escape. (1 Cor.10:13) Friends, be VERY careful when you read WHAT you read. You may want to purchase a good study Bible and Bible commentary. These can be a real help.

WHAT'S YOUR CATERPILLAR?

It was one of the saddest and most traumatic things Marie had seen. I was attending Bethany Bible College in Santa Cruz, California. Marie worked in the front office of Santa Cruz Community Hospital. It was near the end of the work day when it happened. One of Marie's coworkers, a wonderful middle-aged woman with whom Marie was good friends, was walking out the front door when she screamed and ran back into the office, just hysterical.

Something terrifying was inching across the pavement just outside the front door. It took her some time to calm down, at least to explain to Marie what she saw. It was a fuzzy, two-inch caterpillar just minding its own business traveling at about eight inches per minute.

The woman was helplessly and hopelessly terrified of caterpillars. I'm certain that at some point, probably years earlier, she had been exposed to a caterpillar that simply terrified her. Her terror never left. Sound a little absurd? Not to people with this crippling phobia. This wonderful, kind woman lived her whole life, terrified of something that couldn't harm her even if it wanted to. This was absolutely something Marie witnessed first-hand.

Question: Before you answer, think deep. What, if anything, causes you to fear? Maybe not caterpillars. That probably sounds ridiculous. But I wonder, are there things in your life that you fear? Maybe things that someone else might think, "What are they afraid of?"

Isn't God big enough and interested enough to help you conquer your caterpillar? The answer is yes! Put a name on your caterpillar. That's step one. Commit it to God. That's step two. Then face your fear with God's unlimited power and provision. Do it every day if you need to. Several times a day if you need to. Then, please drop me a line and tell me what has changed.

ONE TOUGH COP

His nickname is "Murph." He's a retired tough Gang Unit officer of the Chicago Police Department. His voice is low and gruff, like gravel. He lived with his wife and small dog on Lake Hodstradt about a mile from our cabin in Lake Tomahawk.

We loved stopping by to visit when we went for long walks. You would find him in his gunsmith shop on Poplar Rd. It was a converted three-stall garage on his property. He is well known as an excellent gunsmith in the Northwoods. He also had other weapons of every sort for display or sale. It was a very expensive collection.

Our son Ben and I stopped by one day to say hi and check out his cool stuff. It was interesting for me but utterly fascinating for 12-year-old Ben. Murph's yippy dog was there—his companion. The question begged to be asked so I asked it. "Murph, you don't have a real guard dog. How do you protect the shop from bad guys?"

His answer was as tough and grizzled as he is. I got chills as I listened. "When I first moved up here, I got the word out to the whole area: if you rob me, I will shoot you." Ben looked at me as if to ask, "Dad, is he joking?" My look back at him told the story. There was NO joking with Murph. Needless to say, Murph has NEVER been robbed.

LIKE LIGHTNING FROM HEAVEN

Thinking about Jesus' words in Mark 10:18 "I saw Lucifer falling like lightning from heaven." Some say that one-third of the angels fell with him. But what did Jesus see on that fateful day? I've heard some say that Jesus witnessed the beauty and wonder of this former angel and he was just sharing his experience with His disciples to describe the awesomeness of the one we call Satan.

Yes, He witnessed the awesome spectacle of the one who thought he should be equal with God. But I'm convinced that the description Jesus shared that day had nothing to do with beauty. Friends, what Jesus shared that day had everything to do with the incredible SPEED Lucifer traveled when God said, "Leave My presence.... NOW!"

It happened as lightning displays itself in less than a moment. Bright, powerful, often deadly, and very, very fast!! Yes, Jesus described an all-powerful God with absolutely all authority over all creation. He alone is on heaven's throne and He is King over the whole universe. And He still responds to His people when we pray.

You may feel like Satan is trying to discourage and defeat you. Take heart, dear friends. God is still kicking the enemy out of circumstances. YOUR circumstances!! What you're going through has an end day attached.

God responds to YOUR prayers in His way and in His timing.

SON OF GOD, SON OF MAN

Here's a challenge this Christmas season. Check the New Testament to find all the times the disciples called Jesus "The Son of God." Then, check again to see all the times Jesus referred to himself as "The Son of Man."

You see, the disciples were desperate to convince every person who would listen that Christ was indeed God in the flesh, while Jesus was resolute in identifying himself with mankind.

At one point, Jesus asked them who they thought He was. Remember Peter in Matthew 16:16. "You are the Christ, the Son of the living God." Those around Him said: "Son of God, Son of God, Son of God." They needed to identify with God through His Son.

But one of Jesus' great goals was to identify with mankind. So, he said it again and again: "Son of Man, Son of Man, Son of Man." He GREATLY desired to identify Himself with us!! He WAS one of us!!

HUMAN BRAHMA BULLS

I saw an interesting celebration as I watched football this weekend. It's a celebration I've seen hundreds of times over the last 71 years, and it happens in football at almost every level, particularly in college and pro ball. It happens when a huge running back takes the ball and goes around, over, or through huge defensive linemen to score a touchdown.

Some of these guys seem to be unstoppable as they pound their way into an end zone. Some are huge: 6'3"and 245 pounds. Impressive??? You bet they are. Unstoppable? Sure, seems like it sometimes.

But then one of their offensive guards or tackles runs to celebrate the touchdown and takes that 245-pound wrecking ball and lifts him above his own head like he was a character from *Toy Story*. A wrecking ball celebrating with a 345-pound bulldozer.

What a sight that is for me!! Football has always been a great treat for me. The human Brahma Bulls are a great part of it!!!

Am I alone in this???

WHO PURIFIES THE HEART

Here's a Bible question I think many will miss. Who is it that purifies the heart? Some will answer the Holy Spirit. They would be right. Some will say Jesus who died on the cross so that our sins could be forgiven. They would be right as well. Some will say the Father ... remember what Jesus prayed, "Our Father .... deliver us from evil."

So, all three answers are right. God is the one who purifies the heart. But we've missed a critical part of purifying the heart. James hits it squarely on the head. James 4:8 says, "Cleanse your hands, you sinners, and PURIFY YOUR HEARTS, you double-minded."

Unfortunately, that part of heart purification isn't nearly as popular as the others. Why? Because God's purifying the heart is God doing the work. He purifies, we benefit. Do you see that? But James adds a critical part of the purification process. Does God purify the heart? Of course He does. Does that absolve us of our responsibility to do our part according to James? No, no, no.

And so we pray, "God, purify my heart with the blood of the Lamb. And God, help me to purify my own heart as I am determined to do for your glory!!!

Someone please say, "Amen!" (or "OH ME")

WHO IS GOD TO YOU?

Just a thought for today. It has been said that the perception of God most people in the church understand is what someone else told you about Him. For instance, if you were raised in the Catholic church, your understanding of Him was taught you by a priest or a nun. If you were raised in a Protestant church, your understanding is what you heard from a pastor or Sunday school teacher, or someone else in the church, maybe your parents. Truth is, if you were raised Lutheran, your perception is what the Lutheran church taught you about Him. Likewise, for Baptists, Methodists, Nazarenes, Evangelicals, Pentecostals, and so on.

Many people's understanding of God is based solely on someone else's experience. Teaching and preaching are both good and necessary. But God wants us to draw far closer to Him than someone else's experience. He wants us to have our own connection, our own intimacy, our own personal understanding, not someone else's.

Psalm 34:8 says, "Taste and see that the Lord is good. Blessed is the man who trusts in Him."

Folks, last I looked, the only way to taste something is to internalize it. Have you tasted His presence lately? Chances are if not, you're probably pretty hungry, and you may not even know what you're hungry for. Think about it.

HOW BIG IS YOUR GOD?

Psalm 138:9 says "If I ascend into the heavens, You are there. If I lay down in sheol, You are there."

I want to challenge you with something today. Do we really agree with David that God is truly omnipresent. That He exists everywhere?

Consider this: light travels at 186,000 miles/second. If you could somehow latch onto a beam and ride it for a year, can you imagine how far from Earth you'd be? Well, scientists have determined that the known universe is 94 billion light-years across. That's the distance light would travel (at 186,000 miles/second) in 94 billion years.

Now, hold onto your hats. Is it possible then that He is present at both ends of the universe at exactly the same time? Is it possible that He exists across ALL distance and all time and not just in the space above this tiny planet we call Earth?

OK, get a load of what scientists say is beyond the universe, that is "the Unobserved Universe." Their best observations say that that distance is 23 TRILLION light-years across.

Think God could be at both ends of THAT neighborhood? Kind of puts Psalm 138 in a more realistic light. Do you agree? Have I made your head want to explode? That's not my goal. Just want you to have a realistic understanding of what He's really like.

"IF YOU COME TO A FORK IN THE ROAD, TAKE IT"

This is a quote usually attributed to the great Yogi Berra: "If you come to a fork in the road, take it."

I can hardly remember the hundreds of times people have come to me as their pastor, sincerely wanting my help in making a decision, whether great or small. They had come to a fork in the road, to a place where a decision simply had to be made. Maybe a job opportunity, maybe a large investment such as a home, possibly a relationship decision.

The advice I gave was typically the same. Advice that, if followed diligently, would lead to the right choice. Here it is: When making a decision, whether great or small, ALWAYS empty yourself of self so God's voice is the voice you'll hear. Make the decision truly desiring His will ..... NOTHING MORE, NOTHING LESS, NOTHING ELSE.

If you truly seek His choice at the fork in the road, you can rest fully assured that you'll take the correct branch!! God will honor and bless your road and you'll be able to rest securely in His presence.

CARNIVAL SLAM

Just a small adjustment can make a big difference. Most people who know my brother David and me are not aware of the job we had that summer. I was 14 and David was 15. We went from town to town working at a traveling carnival. The hours were long and we both knew the owner was regularly ripping us off.

We would run the typical attractions: darts at the balloons, the impossible ring toss... (Are those attractions nearly impossible to get one of the large stuffed animals? You bet they are.)

My favorite attraction was the dart board lined with colorful balloons. When someone got lucky and won a prize, it was most often a small toy worth almost nothing. "Hey, we got a really big wiener here." Not winner—*wiener*. Seemed more effective at drawing people in.

Another game I loved to run was the oversized hammer to ring the bell some 25 feet above. I was 14 but I learned how to ring that bell 25 out of 25 attempts. I was strong in those days but not that strong. No, guys much bigger than me would very often fail to ring that stupid bell. Why? It was their technique. Almost every guy would grab that hammer, bring it up over his shoulder., then SMASH. Missed. Missed again ... and again ... you get the picture. The secret? When you swing like you're chopping firewood, that broad hammer will almost never connect straight on the bell catalyst. Thus, you miss much of the connecting power. No, the secret is to bring the hammer directly overhead and POW, you hit the catalyst straight on, with the force of the whole hammerhead. Never fails!!! Just a slight modification brings success, every time.

Are you finding that you're swinging with all YOUR might, but you just can't ring that bell? Whatever the bell is in your life. It may be that God wants to do some modification in you. Maybe nothing real major. Just small changes to put you in proper position with Him. And God is saying..."Child, there's an issue in your life that needs to be modified. Listen to MY voice. Your struggle is not any longer needed."

Friends, what are you struggling with? God is saying, "Bring that hammer directly overhead and let Me direct your attempts. I'll help you to be successful time after time."

How is your hammer swing?

YEAH, BUT IT'S A DRY HEAT!!

"Yeah, but it's a dry heat." I can't say how many times I heard that from family in Milwaukee. When Marie and I lived in the Central Valley (San Joaquin Valley in California), the temperature was often above 100°F in the summer. When I'd call family they would ask the inevitable question, "How hot is it out there?" They may have been sweltering at 85°F in Milwaukee.

I'd answer, "Well, it's 106 right now."

Their answer? You guessed it. "Yeah, but it's a dry heat."

In 1972, that all changed. My parents, two younger brothers, and younger sister Cathy drove all the way from Wisconsin to enjoy our wedding day, June 30th. On the day before the wedding, my siblings got their swim suits on, walked down the steps from my apartment, and headed across the parking lot to take a dip in the pool. I think it was 110°F that day.

Oh, did I mention? They went barefoot just as they would back home. The pavement was probably around 160°F, enough to burn the soles of their feet. They all had to have their feet treated and walked very gingerly the next several days. They were all melting in the blazing California furnace. The result?

I NEVER again heard those infamous words, "Yeah, but it's a dry heat."

By the way, the day of our wedding, it was 112°F. Funny how taking a walk in the furnace changes your mind about the furnace.

THE 87%--13% TRUTH

It's one of those things that sticks in your brain. I heard it from an Oneida council member a number of years back. I took a class with him and we became friends. We got to talking about the Oneida Casino and some of the interesting things about it.

I asked him if he knew how winners compared to losers there. He said, "Just remember these two numbers: 87 and 13. That's how many lose compared to those who win."

I locked those numbers away and never forgot them. He also told me that most people have no idea of the tremendous amounts of money people leave behind every day of the year. In case you're thinking about visiting a casino to make some easy money, remember: 87% of the optimistic visitors come away losers, while 13% are winners.

Just thought I'd pass that along.

YOU'VE GOT ME. WHO'S GOT YOU?

It was one of those movie lines that became a classic. Lois Lane is falling hundreds of feet from a skyscraper. Her death is certain, only moments to live. Then, out of nowhere, the hero appears. He lovingly swoops under her and rescues her from certain disaster. It's Superman!!! "Don't worry, Lois. I've got you." Horrified, she manages to get the now-famous words out. "You've got me!!!! WHO'S GOT YOU??"

I'm guessing it was the pastor/preacher side of me that saw a beautiful parallel between a movie and a real-life hero. One who catches us when we're falling, we're afraid, even terrified. When it feels like there's no help, no answer, nobody who sees our helpless, even hopeless, life circumstances.

When fear surrounds us and, like Lois, we feel that we're about to crash. Nobody sees our predicament. We're falling! It's not that people don't care—it's that they don't KNOW. And we're not sure they'll understand our lonely and fearful life chapter.

"LORD, I'M FALLING AND I'M NOT SURE ANYONE EVEN KNOWS IT!!!"

Here's a word I believe God gave me for some of you, but equally as important, someone you know who needs to hear this. "God, are you really here—for me???"And He wants you to NOT MISS THIS! "Daughter/ Son, I've got you. You won't crash. You won't find disaster. I'm here and I'VE GOT YOU!!'"

But God, who's got YOU??!

"Precious child, let Me take care of that. All you really need to know is, I have surely rescued you."

GOD'S NAME IN VAIN

How did we get this so mixed up? Exodus 20:7 is the 3rd of the Ten Commandments. "You shall not take the name of the Lord your God in vain."

What does that usually mean? Most people would say it's wrong to use God's name as part of a swear word, right? We've heard it all of our lives. "Of course it's right, Dan."

Well, you may be right about that interpretation. But I'm afraid you're not. That's simply not what God was referring to when He delivered the Ten Commandments to Moses.

What does it really mean? I can best explain it with this illustration. Say you and your husband/wife are on vacation at a very nice resort, maybe in Florida. When you purchase a meal, order lemonade at the pool, even shop at one of their boutiques, you simply sign your name and room number. Many nice places don't have you pay at the time of purchase, you have an ongoing tab, paid when your stay is over, usually with a credit or debit card. Nice system.

Marie and I have been fortunate to stay at a number of these places. Here's the issue. Say a lady overhears your wife giving her name and room number at a purchase. She signs the receipt and goes on her merry way. Now, this other woman decides she'd like to do some shopping for new jewelry. She enters a boutique, tries on a beautiful necklace and a diamond tennis bracelet. "I'll take these." She gives the store attendant your WIFE'S NAME and ROOM NUMBER.

"Very good, ma'am. You have a wonderful day and enjoy your jewelry." You can bet she'll enjoy them!! She has taken your wife's name....IN VAIN. She's not who she claims to be. She just benefits from living a lie.

Makes me wonder. How many folks are out there who do the same thing? Taking God's name in vain? They are simply not who they claim to be!! They can be very clever and fool a lot of people. But one day, they will stand before God and have to explain why they did what they did. Of course, God sees immediately through the counterfeit. "HOW IS IT THAT YOU TOOK MY NAME IN VAIN?"

Friends, maybe it's a good time to look deep and reckon with this issue sooner rather than later.

ALL Y'ALL

I think I've finally figured it out!! When someone from the south says, "Y'all," it means "everybody." For example, "Y'all drive home carefully." OK ... I kind of get it. So far so good. But then I heard the plural version, "ALL y'all."

It took a while but I finally figured that one out too. "Y'all" means "everybody" and "All Y'all" means "everybody, plus everybody else."

I had finally unraveled one of the mysteries of the south. It gave me a headache.....

CHEW ON THIS

Something to chew on today. We had friends in Santa Cruz, California who were both on staff at Bethany Bible College. Darrell was a professor. He did his own personal study on books he found at several area Bible book stores. His observation: they all had this in common: 70% of the books focused on people and their problems, while about 30% focused on God and His greatness. Anyone else see some possible imbalance? Just chew on that one today.

COMIC COP

Can you use a good laugh? We spoke with Marie's sister Carolyn in California last night. She'd driven over one of the dangerous mountain passes a day earlier. You've heard about all the snow they've received in the Sierra mountains, measuring in feet, not inches. She passed by a CHP trooper with a great sense of humor. He was standing next to his squad car holding up a large sign that read "FREE SNOW."

I'd love to meet this guy!!!

COUNTERFEIT COWBOYS

I enjoy old cowboy westerns, always have. There are three things that are sadly incorrect in most westerns.

1) Jet vapor trails in the distance. I've seen them in at least seven films.
2) Incorrect depictions of cowboys. Historians say at least 25% of the cowboys were men of color, mostly African American.
3) Finding a watering hole after going days without water on the verge of death. This is one of the worst depictions I've seen. Men on the verge of death bend over or even hop in the water to drink to save their very lives.

But here's where westerns miss reality by a mile. In virtually every depiction, the cowboys take a small drink, then take their hats to dump water over their heads. WRONG!!! A guy on the verge of dying of thirst will get as much fluid into his system as is humanly possible as soon as possible.

What's the big deal, Dan? Here it is: In many 21st century churches, people have grown accustomed to internalizing a gulp of the water Jesus spoke about in John 7:37. "On the last and greatest day of the feast, Jesus stood and said, 'If any man is thirsty, let him come to ME.'"

What we fail to realize is that people are dying of spiritual thirst, but they're not being told that Jesus can quench any and all issues that leave people barely hanging on—with huge rivers of life-sustaining spiritual drink available. We offer a cowboy gulp with the rest staying external, like the cowboy hat poured on the OUTSIDE but not taken on the INSIDE.

GREATEST FANS!!

One question. Who in the WORLD has a scrimmage practice and has 65,000 fans attend??!! In my humble opinion, there are no greater fans in the history of football that even come close to Green Bay Packer fans. Argue if you like, then go try to buy season tickets. (Current waiting time is 60 years...I Googled it)

THIS IS WISCONSIN

It was March 19th. I was driving over the Fox River on Hwy 172. There were some fairly good-sized ice floes floating north toward the bay. The temperature was 22°F. The chill factor was about 5 or 10°F. "Boy, that sure looks cold," I thought to myself.

Then I looked south on the river and guess what I saw. Seven or eight fishing boats on the water apparently dodging the ice floes. Nothing was going to stop those hearty Wisconsin fishermen. I love to fish, but, isn't there a limit on freezing just to catch a walleye? Guess not. This is, after all, Wisconsin.

ZIP ZIP

Could anyone use a good (true) church story laugh today?

A young couple had recently been married. They were getting dressed to go out for one of their first dates as a married couple.

"Honey, would you please zip me up?" asked the sweet wife of her husband. He took the zipper on the back of her new dress and zipped it up, then down, and up and down again. Finally, he zipped it up and they continued to get ready and had a wonderful time that evening.

Jump ahead a few days. The mischievous husband was in the garage working on his car and the wife saw him lying half way under the car. She thought she'd pay him back a little. She snuck up, took the zipper on his Levi's and zipped it up and down as he'd done to her a few days earlier.

"Got him back," she chuckled to herself. Just then, her husband came walking around the side of the garage and said, "HI, honey!" She froze. Almost in despair, she went back into the garage to see who's zipper she'd just played with. It wasn't her husband; he was standing right next to her. Who in the world could it be???!!!

They both went over and the husband called to the man who happened to be an elderly deacon at their church, an auto mechanic. But he wasn't moving. Was he dead??? No, he was so startled when someone did what they did, he tried to sit up, but instead he smacked his forehead on something on the underside of the car, knocking himself out cold.

Don't you know that young bride had some explaining to do!? Again, true story.

WHY SO DOWNCAST?

King David was and is one of the most beloved people in biblical history. His writings in the book of Psalms have encouraged and blessed countless people for 3,500 years. There is a Psalm (actually it's written in at least 2 places) that most don't really fully understand. It's found in both Psalm 42:11 and 43:5. "Why so downcast, O my soul...put your trust in God ."

David was first a shepherd and wrote many of the psalms from a shepherd's perspective. Any shepherd will know what "downcast" means. It speaks of a sheep whose wool has become wet after a rain storm. That wet wool is very heavy. Sheep will lie down in areas where there are small ruts in a field. It's comfortable for a time but it was a dangerously, even deadly position for any sheep to be in.

Lying on its side, the weight of the wet wool prevented the sheep from getting on its feet again—ever. That sheep was "cast down"and could easily die without the shepherd's help.

That's where David got the phrase, "Why so downcast?"or "Why so cast down, O my soul?"

Friends, this still happens all around the world today. People are feeling the weight of conflict all around us. People are feeling the weight of conflict within us, and it can be heavy, more than some can bear. They are down in the dumps—"cast down"and try as they might, they just can't seem to get out of their rut.

David had the answer to his own monolog. "Why so downcast O my soul. PUT YOUR TRUST IN GOD!"

Friends, what is weighing you down, and how long do you need to stay unable to get up from your rut? Three things:

1) Admit you're in a rut.
2) Bleat loud enough for the Shepherd to hear you.
3) Get ready for God to use His shepherd's staff to pull you out to SAFETY and FREEDOM!!

You may want to read Psalms chapters 42 and 43 today.

ALL IN THE PERSPECTIVE

Woke up this morning (May 1st, 2023) and saw the fresh blanket of white snow and thought, "How beautiful it is this morning!"

Then I looked at the calendar and thought, "What a miserable, ugly day!!"

All in the perspective, I suppose.

A GRATEFUL NATION

On behalf of a grateful nation, I would like to thank every man and woman who served in one of our armed forces—and special gratitude for the families who supported their dad, mom, wife, husband, brother, sister, loved one as they served.

We know that some paid the ultimate price. But on this day we set aside to honor all of our heroes, I would like to say a special thanks to all of you who may not have been wounded by a bullet or a bomb, but you still carry awful memories, deep scars, maybe PTSD, as part of your burden. You still carry the wounds people cannot see because you carry them deep inside. Millions of Americans honor you today. But I want to thank you for bearing scars so the rest of us can live free of those scars. We remember you today. We honor and thank you, every day!!

ONE CLEVER COP

Best buddy Scott Koval was a Greenfield, Wisconsin, police lieutenant. He headed their SWAT team and was the city's chief hostage negotiator for some time. He tells the true story of the New York City chief hostage negotiator who'd come to Greenfield for training police officers.

One of the strategies he'd come up with was brilliant. It was the worst possible scenario for any police team. A violent drug addict in New York City had taken his ex-girlfriend hostage in a basement apartment, only one door in or out. It had zero window exposure for the SWAT team to neutralize the bad guy. Negotiations went on for an hour, two hours, four hours, six hours—all night with no progress and hope fading.

Along about 7 the next morning, the training officer came upon a brilliant plan. He told one of his officers to go round up an electric frying pan, some eggs, and a big slab of bacon—and a floor fan. Just down the hall from the worsening situation, one of the officers started cooking breakfast. The fan wafted the delicious aroma of bacon toward the apartment.

After just a few minutes, a gruff voice came through the door. "Hey, what are you guys doing!!?"

Negotiator's response, "We're just having breakfast. Do you want some?"

Pause. "Uh, yeah."

"Come on out, we have plenty."

The door slowly opened and the crisis was over. Instead of throwing the bad guy to the ground and handcuffing him, they had him join them sitting on the floor for a delicious bacon and eggs breakfast.

The New York City cop told Scottie and the other Greenfield officers, "One day, this guy will get out of prison. I want him to know I follow through on my promises." Pretty clever cop, I'd say.

GOLF NUTS

Can you use a good laugh? True story told by a great news and storyteller, Paul Harvey. He began by saying, "This next story is one that only golfers will really understand." Here's the true story."

A man went to his local golf course to meet with some buddies to play 18 holes. While putting his golf shoes on in the parking lot, a thief with a knife confronted him and demanded his wallet. The man, who was not a pushover, got into a tussle with the bad guy. Unfortunately, the thief was able to slice a large wound that cut across his whole palm. Someone approached them and the bad guy ran off. The wound was bleeding badly. He took his golf towel off his bag and wrapped it as tightly as he could, soaking it in blood.

Was he rushed to the hospital? No, he met his friends and played the entire 18-hole golf course with the towel still wrapped around his hand.

Afterwards, he drove himself to the hospital for stiches to close the ugly wound. So Paul Harvey was right—only golfers would understand this story.

DR. NORMAN ARNESON

Something to think about today: My favorite Bible professor at Bethany University in Santa Cruz, California, was Dr. Norman Arneson. He had an incredible gift of exposing the depths of God's Word to students who truly hung on every word he taught, including me. But he was also notorious for including dry and witty humor. He was making a point about all of mankind's position being born of Adam's lineage, therefore in need of blood atonement to make us absolutely acceptable to God.

That is, the blood of God's precious Lamb, His Son Jesus Christ. Then—unless you weren't listening—he threw in this one-liner." Come now, we're all of the same mold (*pregnant pause*), some of us are just moldier than others."

I loved Dr. Arneson's classes.

HOW WOULD YOU ANSWER?

We had good friends back in the early seventies. He was a Spanish teacher in the junior high school, she, a stay-at-home mom. Their daughter was sitting next to her mom on the living room couch. She was a very bright and inquisitive 4-year-old, laser focused on her mom's very pregnant tummy. She was looking for answers.

She posed her mom with a very natural four-year-old's question. "Mom, how's that thing going to get out of there??!!"

Before Mom could come up with an answer that would satisfy the astute four-year-old's brain, the daughter asked an even more challenging question. "Mom, how'd that thing get IN THERE??!!"

I wonder how many would find the right words to satisfy this future big sister?

UNFORGIVENESS

Unforgiveness is like drinking toxic poison and hoping the other guy gets sick.

FASHION-CRAZY

Saw a guy on the news the other day. He had on a sharp black suit, crisp colored shirt, and a tie that matched perfectly. He looked really good until the camera panned down to show his shoes: white, ankle-high basketball shoes. I don't know what brand they were nor did I care.

I have just one question. Am I the only one who thinks that this men's fashion statement is just completely absurd—nuts—ridiculous?

Please drop me a note to let me know that I'm not a fashion porcupine, that I'm not the only one who snickers when I see this latest fashion train wreck.

RON AUCH

He authored 14 books on prayer, spoke around the world, was a pastor, and my good friend. Ron Auch impacted my prayer life more than any other person. Things he planted in my life 40 years ago remain to this day.

One of the truths he shared was short, sweet, but very powerful. He said, "God doesn't want to be Number 3 on your list, He doesn't want to be Number 2 on your list, and He doesn't want to be Number 1 on your list. He wants to be your list."

YIKES!! 1 Corinthians 15:28..."And when all things shall be subdued under Him, then shall the Son also himself be subject unto Him that put all things under Him, that God may be ALL IN ALL."

This challenge has remained with me for 40 years. Ron went to heaven July 11, 2018. I wept many tears that day.

WISCONSIN

Wisconsin is 9 months of winter and 3 months of poor tobogganing. Can I get a witness?

ACKNOWLEDGMENTS

I would like to thank our son Ben for taking my photo for the cover of the book and for editing the audio portion of the book.

Next, I'd like to thank my wife Marie for helping in the process of transferring the files from my tablet and cell phone to the publisher. It was more complicated than I thought it would be.

I would also like to thank my brother David, whose encouragement and support played a great part in tackling the project. He is a rock.

Last, but certainly not least, I'd like to thank my publisher Kira Henschel, whose expert guidance and advice were paramount in making this book. I will forever be grateful to her.

ABOUT THE AUTHOR

Pastor Dan Carlson graduated in 1970 from Milwaukee Hamilton High School with a GPA of 1.9, placing him solidly in the bottom 25% of the class of 975. In seminary, he made the dean's list. Very Unexpected. He then went to work at Ford Aerospace in Palo Alto, California to pay off school bills. Within 10 years of high school graduation, he was appointed Test Conductor in Charge of Launch Operations at Cape Canaveral, Florida. Very unexpected.

As a boy, Dan experienced a very embarrassing and emotionally traumatic speech impediment which got him focused on words, particularly words minus the letter "s" because he could never pronounce "s" correctly. Out of his pain, words became a focal point. Languages became second nature and he studied five, including Spanish, Portuguese, Greek, Hebrew, and English. Very Unexpected.

After Hurricane Katrina, he hand-picked ten Wisconsin professionals to do crisis counseling and debriefings with police officers in New Orleans. They were the first to whom the city allowed access. Very Unexpected.

Dan's entire life has been a series of very unexpected life stories. The hope is that these stories bring you encouragement, hope, spiritual inspiration, and a good belly laugh from time to time.

Pastor Dan's email is: veryunexpected28@gmail.com

www.ingramcontent.com/pod-product-compliance
Lightning Source LLC
Chambersburg PA
CBHW030847090426
42737CB00009B/1138